Instant Pot Cookbook For Beginners 2024

2000 Days of Quick & Easy Instant Pot Magic A Beginner's Handbook to Mastering 2024's Hottest Kitchen Appliance

Kevin S. Smith

Copyright©2023 Kevin S. Smith

All RightReserved...The content of this Book may not be reproduced,replicated or transmitted without written permission from the author or publisher.under no circumstances will any blame or legal responsibility be held against the publisher or the author,for any damages, reparation or monetary due to the information contained in this book.

TABLE OF CONTENTS

Introduction...7
   Getting to Know Your Instant Pot: A Quick Overview. 7
   Tips for Instant Pot Success.................................10

Chapter 1: Breakfast..**15**
   Instant Pot Oatmeal...15
   Instant Pot Egg Casserole....................................16
   Instant Pot Yaourt Parfait......................................16
   Instant Pot Banana Pancakes..............................17
   Instant Pot Breakfast Burritos...............................18
   Instant Pot Blueberry Muffin Bites.........................19
   Instant Pot Breakfast Quinoa Bowl.......................20
   Instant Pot Veggie Frittata.....................................21
   Instant Pot Cinnamon Apple Omelette..................22
   Instant Pot Breakfast Hash...................................23
   Instant Pot Breakfast Rice Pudding......................24
   Instant Pot Breakfast Tacos..................................25
   Instant Pot Breakfast Smoothie Bowl....................25

Chapter 2: Lunch..**27**
   Instant Pot Chicken and Vegetable Soup.............27
   Instant Pot Spaghetti Bolognese..........................28
   Instant Pot Quinoa and Black Bean Bowl............29
   Instant Pot Chicken Burrito Bowls........................30
   Instant Pot Lentil Soup..31
      Instant Pot Shrimp and Broccoli Stir-Fry...........32

Instant Pot Butternut Squash Risotto.....................33
Instant Pot Turkey Chili..35
Instant Pot Coconut Curry Chicken........................ 36
Instant Pot Cauliflower and Chickpea Curry...........37
Instant Pot Beef and Broccoli.................................. 38
Instant Pot Lemon Garlic Chicken...........................39

Chapter 3: Dinner.. 42
Instant Pot Chicken Alfredo Pasta...........................42
Instant Pot Beef Stew... 43
Instant Pot Vegetarian Chili..................................... 44
Instant Pot Teriyaki Chicken.................................... 45
Instant Pot Lemon Herb Salmon..............................46
Instant Pot BBQ Pulled Pork....................................47
Instant Pot Ratatouille...48
Instant Pot Beef and Broccoli Stir-Fry.....................50
Instant Pot Stuffed Bell Peppers..............................51
Instant Pot Chicken Curry...52
Instant Pot Mushroom and Spinach Risotto........... 53

Chapter 4: Appetizers Soups and Sides.................. 55
Instant Pot Spinach and Artichoke Dip....................55
Instant Pot Tomato Basil Soup.................................56
Instant Pot Buffalo Cauliflower Bites.......................57
Instant Pot Loaded Baked Potato Soup.................. 58
Instant Pot Caprese Salad Skewers........................59
Instant Pot Garlic Parmesan Brussels Sprouts.......60
Instant Pot Creamy Corn Dip...................................61
Instant Pot Sweet Potato Fries................................ 62
Instant Pot Greek Salad...63

Instant Pot Buttery Garlic Knots..............................64

Chapter 5: Vegan and Vegetarian............................66
Instant Pot Lentil Soup (Vegan)..............................66
Instant Pot Chickpea and Spinach Curry (Vegan)..67
Instant Pot Vegetable Paella (Vegetarian)..............68
Instant Pot Black Bean Chili (Vegan).......................69
Instant Pot Eggplant and Chickpea Stew (Vegan)..71
Instant Pot Quinoa and Vegetable Stir-Fry (Vegetarian)...72
Instant Pot Sweet Potato and Chickpea Curry (Vegan)...73
Instant Pot Mushroom Risotto (Vegetarian)............74
Instant Pot Red Lentil Curry (Vegan).......................75
Instant Pot Cauliflower and Chickpea Curry (Vegan). 77

Chapter 6: Fish and Seafoods...................................80
Instant Pot Lemon Garlic Butter Shrimp.................80
Instant Pot Garlic Herb Salmon...............................81
Instant Pot Cajun Shrimp and Sausage Jambalaya... 82
Instant Pot Coconut-Lime Cod Fish Tacos.............83
Instant Pot Seafood Paella.......................................84
Instant Pot Teriyaki Salmon Bowl............................85
Instant Pot Garlic Lemon Butter Scallops...............87
Instant Pot Thai Coconut Shrimp Soup..................88
Instant Pot Lemon Dill Cod Filets............................89
Instant Pot Spicy Garlic Butter Lobster Tails..........90

Chapter 7: Dessert and Drinks................................92
Instant Pot Chocolate Lava Cake...........................92

Instant Pot Vanilla Rice Pudding...............................93
Instant Pot Apple Crisp..94
Instant Pot Chocolate Cheesecake........................95
Instant Pot Lemon Blueberry Bread Pudding......... 97
Instant Pot Cherry Almond Clafoutis.......................99
Instant Pot Caramel Pecan Cheesecake..............101
Instant Pot Mint Chocolate Cheesecake...............103
Instant Pot Iced Caramel Macchiato.....................105
Conclusion... 106

INTRODUCTION

In the ever-evolving landscape of modern kitchens, the Instant Pot has emerged as a revolutionary appliance, transforming the way we approach home cooking. Gone are the days of spending hours in the kitchen to prepare a wholesome meal. The Instant Pot, often referred to as a multi-functional electric pressure cooker, has become a staple for both novice and seasoned cooks alike. This chapter serves as a warm welcome to the Instant Pot revolution, providing an introduction to this remarkable kitchen companion and laying the groundwork for a culinary adventure.

Getting to Know Your Instant Pot: A Quick Overview

Unveiling the Instant Pot
Upon unboxing your Instant Pot, you're met with a sleek, modern appliance that combines several kitchen gadgets into one.

The device typically includes a stainless steel inner pot, a sealing ring, a steam rack, and various cooking programs. Understanding the components and their functions is key to unlocking the full potential of your Instant Pot.

Instant Pot Models and Variations

The Instant Pot family has expanded over the years, offering various models with unique features to cater to different cooking needs. Whether you have the Instant Pot Duo, Lux, Ultra, or a more advanced model, this section provides an overview of the differences and similarities, helping you navigate the options available in 2024.

The Science Behind Instant Pot Cooking

To truly appreciate the Instant Pot, it's essential to grasp the science behind its cooking methods. The appliance utilizes a combination of pressure and steam to accelerate the cooking process, resulting in faster and more efficient meals. This section delves into the principles of pressure cooking, explaining how it enhances flavors and tenderizes tough cuts of meat.

Instant Pot Buttons and Functions

While the Instant Pot may seem intimidating with its array of buttons, each one serves a specific purpose to simplify your cooking experience. From "Pressure Cook" to "Sauté" and "Keep Warm," this section breaks down the functions, ensuring you're equipped to confidently select the right setting for your recipes.

Essential Instant Pot Accessories

Enhancing your Instant Pot experience goes beyond understanding the appliance itself. Discovering the array of accessories available can take your cooking to the next level. From silicone sealing rings to steam baskets and extra inner pots, this section explores the must-have accessories that will make your Instant Pot a versatile kitchen workhorse.

Tips for Instant Pot Success

Start with Simple Recipes

For Instant Pot beginners, embarking on your culinary journey with straightforward recipes is a wise approach. Mastering the basics, such as cooking rice, preparing soups, or making hard-boiled eggs, allows you to become familiar with the Instant Pot's functionality without feeling overwhelmed. As you gain confidence, you can gradually tackle more complex dishes.

Embrace the Quick and Efficient Cooking

One of the Instant Pot's most appealing features is its ability to significantly reduce cooking time. Embrace the speed and efficiency of pressure cooking, as it not only saves time but also helps retain the nutritional value of your ingredients. Say goodbye to lengthy hours in the kitchen and welcome to quick, tasty dinners.

Use the Instant Pot for Meal Prep

Efficient meal prep is a game-changer for busy individuals and families. The Instant

Pot excels at batch cooking, allowing you to prepare large quantities of food that can be portioned and stored for later use. From hearty stews to tender proteins, meal prep becomes a breeze with the Instant Pot by your side.

Learn the Art of Natural Pressure Release

Understanding when to use natural pressure release (NPR) versus quick pressure release (QPR) is a crucial aspect of Instant Pot cooking. NPR involves letting the built-up pressure release naturally, which is ideal for delicate foods like rice or certain cuts of meat. On the other hand, QPR is suitable for recipes where you want to stop the cooking process immediately.

Experiment with Flavors and Ingredients

The Instant Pot is a versatile canvas for culinary creativity. Don't be scared to try various flavors, spices, and ingredients.Whether you're adapting traditional recipes or creating entirely new ones, the Instant Pot's sealed environment intensifies flavors, resulting in dishes that are both rich and nuanced.

Take Advantage of Pre-Programmed Settings

Many Instant Pot models come equipped with pre-programmed settings for specific dishes such as soup, rice, and poultry. These settings take the guesswork out of cooking times and temperatures, making it even easier for beginners to achieve excellent results. Familiarize yourself with these settings and use them as a starting point for your culinary endeavors.

Mastering Sautéing and Browning

The Instant Pot's sauté function adds an extra layer of versatility to the appliance. Perfect for browning meat, sautéing aromatics, or reducing sauces, this feature allows you to complete multiple cooking steps in a single pot. Understanding the nuances of sautéing in the Instant Pot enhances the depth of flavor in your dishes.

Keep the Sealing Ring in Top Condition

The sealing ring is a crucial component of the Instant Pot, ensuring a tight seal during the cooking process. Regular maintenance, such as removing and cleaning the sealing ring after each use, is essential to prevent odors and maintain optimal performance. Additionally, having a spare sealing ring on hand can be convenient for preventing cross-flavors in sweet and savory dishes.

Adjusting Recipes for the Instant Pot

Adapting traditional recipes for the Instant Pot requires some adjustments, but it's a skill worth mastering. Factors such as cooking times, liquid ratios, and the order of ingredients may need modification. This section provides valuable insights into how to convert your favorite recipes for successful Instant Pot cooking.

Stay Patient and Enjoy the Learning Process

As with any new skill, there may be a learning curve when you first start using the Instant Pot. Be patient with yourself, and enjoy the learning process. Each cooking experience, whether a triumph or a learning opportunity, contributes to your growing mastery of this innovative kitchen tool.

As you embark on your Instant Pot journey, remember that this revolutionary appliance is designed to simplify and enhance your cooking experience. From understanding the basics to mastering advanced techniques, the Instant Pot opens up a world of culinary possibilities. Armed with the knowledge from this chapter, you're well-equipped to dive into the exciting realm of Instant Pot cooking, where quick and easy magic happens in every dish.

CHAPTER 1: BREAKFAST

Instant Pot Oatmeal

Ingredients:
- 1 cup rolled oats
- 2 cups water or milk
- 1/2 teaspoon cinnamon
- Pinch of salt
- Toppings: sliced bananas, berries, honey, and nuts

Instructions:
- Combine oats, water or milk, cinnamon, and salt in the Instant Pot.
- Set Instant Pot to "Porridge" mode and cook for 3 minutes.
- Allow natural pressure release for 5 minutes, then quick release.
- Serve with your favorite toppings.

Prep Time: 2 minutes
Cook Time: 8 minutes
Nutritional Value: High in fiber, protein, and essential nutrients.

Instant Pot Egg Casserole

Ingredients:
- 6 eggs, beaten
- 1 cup diced ham or cooked sausage
- 1 cup shredded cheddar cheese
- 1 cup diced bell peppers
- Salt and pepper to taste

Instructions:
- Grease the Instant Pot insert.
- In a bowl, mix beaten eggs, ham or sausage, cheese, bell peppers, salt, and pepper.
- Pour the mixture into the Instant Pot.
- Set to "Manual" for 8 minutes.
- Quick release and let it sit for 2 minutes before serving.

Prep Time: 10 minutes
Cook Time: 8 minutes
Nutritional Value: High in protein and calcium.

Instant Pot Yaourt Parfait

Ingredients:

- 2 cups Greek yogurt
- 1 cup granola
- 1 cup mixed berries
- 2 tablespoons honey

Instructions:
- Spoon Greek yogurt into serving bowls.
- Top with granola, mixed berries, and drizzle with honey.
- Serve immediately.

Prep Time: 5 minutes
Cook Time: 0 minutes
Nutritional Value: Rich in probiotics, fiber, and antioxidants.

Instant Pot Banana Pancakes

Ingredients:
- 2 ripe bananas, mashed
- 2 eggs
- 1 cup milk
- 1 1/2 cups pancake mix
- 1 teaspoon vanilla extract

Instructions:
- In a bowl, combine mashed bananas, eggs, milk, pancake mix, and vanilla extract.
- Grease the Instant Pot insert.
- Pour the batter into the Instant Pot.
- Set to "Sauté" mode and cook pancakes on both sides.

Prep Time: 10 minutes
Cook Time: 10 minutes
Nutritional Value: Good source of potassium and energy.

Instant Pot Breakfast Burritos

Ingredients:
- 4 large eggs, scrambled
- 1 cup cooked and seasoned black beans
- 1 cup diced tomatoes
- 1 cup shredded cheese
- 4 large flour tortillas

Instructions:

- In the Instant Pot, cook scrambled eggs using the "Sauté" mode.
- Assemble burritos with eggs, black beans, tomatoes, and cheese.
- Wrap each burrito in a tortilla.
- Set to "Manual" for 3 minutes.

Prep Time: 15 minutes
Cook Time: 3 minutes
Nutritional Value: Protein-packed and high in fiber.

Instant Pot Blueberry Muffin Bites

Ingredients:
- 1 cup blueberries
- 2 cups pancake mix
- 1 cup milk
- 1/4 cup melted butter
- 1/4 cup maple syrup

Instructions:
- In a bowl, mix blueberries, pancake mix, milk, melted butter, and maple syrup.
- Grease the Instant Pot silicone molds.

- Pour the batter into the molds.
- Set to "Steam" for 10 minutes.

Prep Time: 10 minutes
Cook Time: 10 minutes
Nutritional Value: Rich in antioxidants and energy.

Instant Pot Breakfast Quinoa Bowl

Ingredients:
- 1 cup quinoa, rinsed
- 2 cups almond milk
- 1/2 cup dried cranberries
- 1/4 cup chopped nuts
- 1 tablespoon honey

Instructions:
- Combine quinoa, almond milk, dried cranberries, and chopped nuts in the Instant Pot.
- Set to "Porridge" mode and cook for 5 minutes.
- Allow natural pressure release for 5 minutes.

- Drizzle with honey before serving.

Prep Time: 5 minutes
Cook Time: 10 minutes
Nutritional Value: High in protein, fiber, and antioxidants.

Instant Pot Veggie Frittata

Ingredients:
- 6 eggs, beaten
- 1 cup diced bell peppers
- 1 cup cherry tomatoes, halved
- 1 cup chopped spinach
- Salt and pepper to taste

Instructions:

Grease the Instant Pot insert.
- In a bowl, mix beaten eggs, bell peppers, tomatoes, spinach, salt, and pepper.
- Pour the mixture into the Instant Pot.
- Set to "Manual" for 5 minutes.
- Quick release and let it sit for 2 minutes before serving.

Prep Time: 15 minutes

Cook Time: 5 minutes

Nutritional Value: High in vitamins and protein.

Instant Pot Cinnamon Apple Omelette

Ingredients:
- 4 eggs, beaten
- 1 apple, peeled and diced
- 1 tablespoon butter
- 1 teaspoon cinnamon
- 1/4 cup chopped walnuts

Instructions:
- In the Instant Pot, cook diced apples with butter and cinnamon using the "Sauté" mode.
- Remove apples and set aside.
- Grease the Instant Pot insert.
- Pour beaten eggs into the pot.
- As eggs set, add cooked apples and chopped walnuts.
- Fold the omelet and cook until eggs are fully set.

Prep Time: 10 minutes
Cook Time: 10 minutes
Nutritional Value: Rich in fiber, vitamins, and healthy fats.

Instant Pot Breakfast Hash

Ingredients:
- 2 cups diced potatoes
- 1 cup diced bell peppers
- 1 cup diced ham
- 1 cup shredded cheddar cheese
- 4 eggs

Instructions:
- Grease the Instant Pot insert.
- Layer diced potatoes, bell peppers, ham, and cheese.
- Create wells in the mixture and crack an egg into each well.
- Set to "Manual" for 8 minutes.
- Quick release and serve.

Prep Time: 15 minutes
Cook Time: 8 minutes

Nutritional Value: High in protein and a good source of vitamins.

Instant Pot Breakfast Rice Pudding

Ingredients:
- 1 cup jasmine rice, rinsed
- 2 cups milk
- 1/4 cup sugar
- 1 teaspoon vanilla extract
- 1/2 cup raisins

Instructions:
- Combine rice, milk, sugar, vanilla extract, and raisins in the Instant Pot.
- Set to "Porridge" mode and cook for 10 minutes.
- Allow natural pressure release for 5 minutes.
- Stir before serving.

Prep Time: 5 minutes
Cook Time: 15 minutes
Nutritional Value: A comforting source of energy.

Instant Pot Breakfast Tacos

Ingredients:
- 4 large eggs, scrambled
- 1 cup black beans, cooked and seasoned
- 1 cup diced avocado
- 1/2 cup salsa
- 4 small tortillas

Instructions:
- In the Instant Pot, cook scrambled eggs using the "Sauté" mode.
- Assemble tacos with eggs, black beans, diced avocado, and salsa.
- Warm tortillas using the "Steam" function.

Prep Time: 10 minutes
Cook Time: 5 minutes
Nutritional Value: A balance of protein, fiber, and healthy fats.

Instant Pot Breakfast Smoothie Bowl

Ingredients:
- 2 frozen bananas
- 1 cup frozen mixed berries
- 1 cup Greek yogurt
- 1/2 cup almond milk
- Toppings: granola, chia seeds, and sliced strawberries

Instructions:
- Blend frozen bananas, mixed berries, Greek yogurt, and almond milk until smooth.
- Pour the smoothie into bowls.
- Top with granola, chia seeds, and sliced strawberries.

Prep Time: 5 minutes
Cook Time: 0 minutes
Nutritional Value: Packed with vitamins, probiotics, and antioxidants.

CHAPTER 2: LUNCH

Instant Pot Chicken and Vegetable Soup

Ingredients:
- 1 lb boneless, skinless chicken thighs
- 4 cups chicken broth
- 2 carrots, sliced
- 2 celery stalks, chopped
- 1 onion, diced
- 1 cup frozen peas
- 2 cloves garlic, minced
- 1 teaspoon dried thyme
- Salt and pepper to taste

Instructions:
- Place chicken thighs, chicken broth, carrots, celery, onion, peas, garlic, thyme, salt, and pepper in the Instant Pot.
- Set to "Soup" mode for 15 minutes.
- Quick release and shred the cooked chicken before serving.

Prep Time: 15 minutes
Cook Time: 15 minutes
Nutritional Value: High in protein, vitamins, and fiber.

Instant Pot Spaghetti Bolognese

Ingredients:
- 1 lb ground beef
- 1 onion, diced
- 2 cloves garlic, minced
- 2 cups tomato sauce
- 1 teaspoon dried oregano
- 1 teaspoon dried basil
- Salt and pepper to taste
- 1 lb spaghetti

Instructions:
- Set Instant Pot to "Sauté" and cook ground beef until browned.
- Add onion and garlic, sauté until softened.
- Stir in tomato sauce, oregano, basil, salt, and pepper.

- Break spaghetti in half and layer on top.
- Set to "Manual" for 8 minutes.

Prep Time: 10 minutes
Cook Time: 8 minutes
Nutritional Value: Rich in protein, iron, and fiber.

Instant Pot Quinoa and Black Bean Bowl

Ingredients:
- 1 cup quinoa, rinsed
- 2 cups vegetable broth
- 1 can black beans, drained and rinsed
- 1 cup corn kernels
- 1 bell pepper, diced
- 1 teaspoon cumin
- 1 teaspoon chili powder
- Salt and pepper to taste
- Avocado for garnish

Instructions:

- Combine quinoa, vegetable broth, black beans, corn, bell pepper, cumin, chili powder, salt, and pepper in the Instant Pot.
- Set to "Manual" for 5 minutes.
- Quick release and fluff quinoa with a fork.
- Serve with sliced avocado.

Prep Time: 10 minutes
Cook Time: 5 minutes
Nutritional Value: High in protein, fiber, and vitamins.

Instant Pot Chicken Burrito Bowls

Ingredients:
- 1 lb chicken breasts, diced
- 1 cup rice
- 1 can black beans, drained and rinsed
- 1 cup corn kernels
- 1 cup salsa
- 1 teaspoon cumin
- 1 teaspoon chili powder
- Salt and pepper to taste

- Shredded cheese and cilantro for garnish

Instructions:
- Place chicken, rice, black beans, corn, salsa, cumin, chili powder, salt, and pepper in the Instant Pot.
- Set to "Manual" for 10 minutes.
- Quickly release the rice and fluff it with a fork.
- Serve with shredded cheese and cilantro.

Prep Time: 15 minutes
Cook Time: 10 minutes
Nutritional Value: Protein-packed with a mix of carbohydrates and veggies.

Instant Pot Lentil Soup

Ingredients:
- 1 cup dried lentils, rinsed
- 4 cups vegetable broth
- 1 onion, diced
- 2 carrots, sliced
- 2 celery stalks, chopped

- 2 cloves garlic, minced
- 1 teaspoon cumin
- 1 teaspoon paprika
- Salt and pepper to taste
- Fresh parsley for garnish

Instructions:
- Combine lentils, vegetable broth, onion, carrots, celery, garlic, cumin, paprika, salt, and pepper in the Instant Pot.
- Set to "Soup" mode for 15 minutes.
- Natural pressure release and garnish with fresh parsley before serving.

Prep Time: 10 minutes
Cook Time: 15 minutes
Nutritional Value: High in fiber, iron, and vitamins.

Instant Pot Shrimp and Broccoli Stir-Fry

Ingredients:
- 1 lb shrimp, peeled and deveined
- 3 cups broccoli florets
- 1 bell pepper, sliced

- 2 tablespoons soy sauce
- 1 tablespoon oyster sauce
- 1 teaspoon sesame oil
- 2 cloves garlic, minced
- 1 teaspoon ginger, grated
- Cooked rice for serving

Instructions:
- Set Instant Pot to "Sauté" and cook shrimp until pink.
- Add broccoli, bell pepper, soy sauce, oyster sauce, sesame oil, garlic, and ginger.
- Stir and set to "Manual" for 2 minutes.
- Quick release and serve over cooked rice.

Prep Time: 15 minutes
Cook Time: 2 minutes
Nutritional Value: Low in calories and rich in protein.

Instant Pot Butternut Squash Risotto

Ingredients:

- 1 cup Arborio rice
- 2 cups butternut squash, diced
- 4 cups vegetable broth
- 1 onion, diced
- 2 cloves garlic, minced
- 1/2 cup Parmesan cheese, grated
- 2 tablespoons olive oil
- Salt and pepper to taste

Instructions:

- Set Instant Pot to "Sauté" and cook onion and garlic in olive oil until softened.
- Add Arborio rice, butternut squash, vegetable broth, salt, and pepper.
- Set to "Manual" for 6 minutes.
- Quick release and stir in Parmesan cheese before serving.

Prep Time: 20 minutes
Cook Time: 6 minutes
Nutritional Value: Creamy and rich in vitamins.

Instant Pot Turkey Chili

Ingredients:
- 1 lb ground turkey
- 1 onion, diced
- 2 bell peppers, diced
- 2 cans diced tomatoes
- 1 can kidney beans, drained and rinsed
- 1 can black beans, drained and rinsed
- 2 tablespoons chili powder
- 1 teaspoon cumin
- Salt and pepper to taste
- Sour cream and shredded cheese for topping

Instructions:
- Set Instant Pot to "Sauté" and cook ground turkey until browned.
- Add onion, bell peppers, diced tomatoes, kidney beans, black beans, chili powder, cumin, salt, and pepper.
- Set to "Manual" for 10 minutes.
- Quick release and serve with sour cream and shredded cheese.

Prep Time: 15 minutes
Cook Time: 10 minutes
Nutritional Value: High in protein, fiber, and essential nutrients.

Instant Pot Coconut Curry Chicken

Ingredients:
- 1.5 lbs chicken thighs, diced
- 1 can coconut milk
- 1 onion, diced
- 2 bell peppers, sliced
- 2 tablespoons red curry paste
- 1 tablespoon fish sauce
- 1 tablespoon soy sauce
- 1 tablespoon brown sugar
- Fresh cilantro for garnish

Instructions:
- Set Instant Pot to "Sauté" and cook chicken until browned.
- Add coconut milk, onion, bell peppers, red curry paste, fish sauce, soy sauce, and brown sugar.

- Set to "Manual" for 8 minutes.
- Natural pressure release, then garnish with fresh cilantro.

Prep Time: 20 minutes
Cook Time: 8 minutes
Nutritional Value: Rich in flavor and high-quality protein.

Instant Pot Cauliflower and Chickpea Curry

Ingredients:
- 1 head cauliflower, cut into florets
- 1 can chickpeas, drained and rinsed
- 1 onion, diced
- 2 cloves garlic, minced
- 1 can diced tomatoes
- 1 can coconut milk
- 2 tablespoons curry powder
- 1 teaspoon turmeric
- Salt and pepper to taste
- Fresh cilantro for garnish

Instructions:

- Set Instant Pot to "Sauté" and cook onion and garlic until softened.
- Add cauliflower, chickpeas, diced tomatoes, coconut milk, curry powder, turmeric, salt, and pepper.
- Set to "Manual" for 5 minutes.
- Quick release and garnish with fresh cilantro.

Prep Time: 15 minutes
Cook Time: 5 minutes
Nutritional Value: Plant-based and rich in fiber.

Instant Pot Beef and Broccoli

Ingredients:
- 1 lb flank steak, sliced
- 3 cups broccoli florets
- 1/2 cup soy sauce
- 1/4 cup hoisin sauce
- 2 tablespoons brown sugar
- 2 cloves garlic, minced
- 1 teaspoon ginger, grated
- Sesame seeds for garnish

Instructions:
- Set Instant Pot to "Sauté" and cook sliced flank steak until browned.
- Add broccoli, soy sauce, hoisin sauce, brown sugar, garlic, and ginger.
- Set to "Manual" for 4 minutes.
- Quick release and garnish with sesame seeds.
- Prep Time: 20 minutes

Cook Time: 4 minutes

Nutritional Value: High in protein and essential minerals.

Instant Pot Lemon Garlic Chicken

Ingredients:
- 1.5 lbs chicken thighs, bone-in
- 1 lemon, sliced
- 4 cloves garlic, minced
- 1 teaspoon dried thyme
- 1 teaspoon dried rosemary
- 1/2 cup chicken broth
- Salt and pepper to taste

- Fresh parsley for garnish

Instructions:
- Season chicken thighs with salt, pepper, thyme, and rosemary.
- Place chicken in the Instant Pot and top with lemon slices and minced garlic.
- Pour chicken broth over the top.
- Set to "Manual" for 10 minutes.
- Natural pressure release and garnish with fresh parsley.

Prep Time: 15 minutes
Cook Time: 10 minutes
Nutritional Value: Juicy and flavorful with a boost of vitamin C.

Instant Pot Mushroom Risotto

Ingredients:
- 1 cup Arborio rice
- 2 cups mushrooms, sliced
- 4 cups vegetable broth
- 1 onion, diced
- 2 cloves garlic, minced
- 1/2 cup dry white wine

- 2 tablespoons olive oil
- Salt and pepper to taste
- Grated Parmesan cheese for garnish

Instructions:
- Set Instant Pot to "Sauté" and cook onion and garlic in olive oil until softened.
- Add mushrooms and continue to sauté until browned.
- Pour in Arborio rice and stir.
- Deglaze with white wine, then add vegetable broth, salt, and pepper.
- Set to "Manual" for 6 minutes.
- Quick release and serve with grated Parmesan cheese.

Prep Time: 20 minutes
Cook Time: 6 minutes
Nutritional Value: Creamy and satisfying with a rich umami flavor.

CHAPTER 3: DINNER

Instant Pot Chicken Alfredo Pasta

Ingredients:
- 1 lb boneless, skinless chicken breasts, diced
- 2 cups fettuccine pasta
- 2 cups chicken broth
- 1 cup heavy cream
- 1 cup grated Parmesan cheese
- 2 tablespoons butter
- 2 cloves garlic, minced
- Salt and pepper to taste
- Fresh parsley for garnish

Instructions:
- Set Instant Pot to "Sauté" and cook diced chicken until browned.
- Add fettuccine pasta, chicken broth, heavy cream, Parmesan cheese, butter, garlic, salt, and pepper.
- Set to "Manual" for 6 minutes.

- Quick release and garnish with fresh parsley before serving.

Prep Time: 15 minutes
Cook Time: 6 minutes
Nutritional Value: Creamy and rich in protein.

Instant Pot Beef Stew

Ingredients:
- 1.5 lbs stew beef, cubed
- 4 cups beef broth
- 1 onion, diced
- 3 carrots, sliced
- 3 potatoes, diced
- 2 cloves garlic, minced
- 1 teaspoon dried thyme
- 1 teaspoon paprika
- Salt and pepper to taste
- Fresh parsley for garnish

Instructions:
- Set Instant Pot to "Sauté" and brown stew beef.

- Add beef broth, onion, carrots, potatoes, garlic, thyme, paprika, salt, and pepper.
- Set to "Stew" mode for 20 minutes.
- Natural pressure release and garnish with fresh parsley.

Prep Time: 20 minutes
Cook Time: 20 minutes
Nutritional Value: Hearty and high in protein.

Instant Pot Vegetarian Chili

Ingredients:
- 2 cans black beans, drained and rinsed
- 1 can kidney beans, drained and rinsed
- 1 can diced tomatoes
- 1 cup corn kernels
- 1 onion, diced
- 2 bell peppers, diced
- 2 cloves garlic, minced
- 2 tablespoons chili powder
- 1 teaspoon cumin

- Salt and pepper to taste
- Avocado and shredded cheese for topping

Instructions:
- Combine black beans, kidney beans, diced tomatoes, corn, onion, bell peppers, garlic, chili powder, cumin, salt, and pepper in the Instant Pot.
- Set to "Manual" for 10 minutes.
- Quick release and serve with sliced avocado and shredded cheese.

Prep Time: 15 minutes
Cook Time: 10 minutes
Nutritional Value: High in fiber, vitamins, and plant-based protein.

Instant Pot Teriyaki Chicken

Ingredients:
- 1.5 lbs chicken thighs, boneless and skinless
- 1/2 cup soy sauce
- 1/4 cup honey
- 2 tablespoons rice vinegar

- 1 tablespoon ginger, grated
- 2 cloves garlic, minced
- 1 tablespoon cornstarch
- Sesame seeds and green onions for garnish

Instructions:
- Place chicken thighs in the Instant Pot.
- In a bowl, mix soy sauce, honey, rice vinegar, ginger, garlic, and cornstarch.
- Pour the sauce over the chicken.
- Set to "Manual" for 8 minutes.
- Quick release and garnish with sesame seeds and green onions.

Prep Time: 15 minutes
Cook Time: 8 minutes
Nutritional Value: Sweet and savory, high in protein.

Instant Pot Lemon Herb Salmon

Ingredients:
- 4 salmon filets
- 1/4 cup olive oil

- 2 tablespoons lemon juice
- 1 teaspoon dried dill
- 1 teaspoon dried thyme
- 2 cloves garlic, minced
- Salt and pepper to taste
- Lemon slices for garnish

Instructions:
- In a bowl, mix olive oil, lemon juice, dill, thyme, garlic, salt, and pepper.
- Place salmon filets in the Instant Pot and pour the marinade over them.
- Set to "Manual" for 3 minutes.
- Quick release and garnish with lemon slices.

Prep Time: 10 minutes
Cook Time: 3 minutes
Nutritional Value: Rich in omega-3 fatty acids.

Instant Pot BBQ Pulled Pork

Ingredients:
- 2 lbs pork shoulder, trimmed and cubed

- 1 cup barbecue sauce
- 1/2 cup chicken broth
- 1 onion, diced
- 2 cloves garlic, minced
- 1 teaspoon smoked paprika
- 1 teaspoon cumin
- Salt and pepper to taste
- Burger buns for serving

Instructions:
- Set Instant Pot to "Sauté" and brown pork cubes.
- Add barbecue sauce, chicken broth, onion, garlic, smoked paprika, cumin, salt, and pepper.
- Set to "Manual" for 45 minutes.
- Natural pressure release and shred pork with two forks.
- Serve on burger buns.

Prep Time: 20 minutes
Cook Time: 45 minutes
Nutritional Value: High in protein, smokey and flavorful.

Instant Pot Ratatouille

Ingredients:
- 1 eggplant, diced
- 2 zucchini, sliced
- 1 bell pepper, diced
- 1 onion, diced
- 2 cloves garlic, minced
- 1 can diced tomatoes
- 2 tablespoons tomato paste
- 1 teaspoon dried thyme
- 1 teaspoon dried rosemary
- Salt and pepper to taste
- Fresh basil for garnish

Instructions:
- Combine eggplant, zucchini, bell pepper, onion, garlic, diced tomatoes, tomato paste, thyme, rosemary, salt, and pepper in the Instant Pot.
- Set to "Manual" for 8 minutes.
- Quick release and garnish with fresh basil.

Prep Time: 15 minutes
Cook Time: 8 minutes

Nutritional Value: Low-calorie and rich in vitamins.

Instant Pot Beef and Broccoli Stir-Fry

Ingredients:
- 1 lb flank steak, sliced
- 3 cups broccoli florets
- 1 bell pepper, sliced
- 2 tablespoons soy sauce
- 1 tablespoon oyster sauce
- 1 tablespoon sesame oil
- 2 cloves garlic, minced
- 1 teaspoon ginger, grated
- Cooked rice for serving

Instructions:
- Set Instant Pot to "Sauté" and cook sliced flank steak until browned.
- Add broccoli, bell pepper, soy sauce, oyster sauce, sesame oil, garlic, and ginger.
- Stir and set to "Manual" for 2 minutes.

- Quick release and serve over cooked rice.

Prep Time: 15 minutes
Cook Time: 2 minutes
Nutritional Value: Low in calories and rich in protein.

Instant Pot Stuffed Bell Peppers

Ingredients:
- 4 bell peppers, halved and seeds removed
- 1 lb ground beef
- 1 cup cooked rice
- 1 can diced tomatoes
- 1 onion, diced
- 2 cloves garlic, minced
- 1 teaspoon Italian seasoning
- Salt and pepper to taste
- Shredded cheese for topping

Instructions:
- Set Instant Pot to "Sauté" and cook ground beef until browned.

- Add cooked rice, diced tomatoes, onion, garlic, Italian seasoning, salt, and pepper.
- Stuffed bell pepper halves with the mixture.
- Set to "Manual" for 8 minutes.
- Quick release and sprinkle shredded cheese on top.

Prep Time: 20 minutes
Cook Time: 8 minutes
Nutritional Value: Protein-packed and a good source of vitamins.

Instant Pot Chicken Curry

Ingredients:
- 1.5 lbs chicken thighs, bone-in
- 1 can coconut milk
- 1 onion, diced
- 2 bell peppers, sliced
- 2 tablespoons red curry paste
- 1 tablespoon fish sauce
- 1 tablespoon soy sauce
- 1 tablespoon brown sugar

- Fresh cilantro for garnish

Instructions:
- Set Instant Pot to "Sauté" and cook chicken until browned.
- Add coconut milk, onion, bell peppers, red curry paste, fish sauce, soy sauce, and brown sugar.
- Set to "Manual" for 8 minutes.
- Natural pressure release and garnish with fresh cilantro.

Prep Time: 20 minutes
Cook Time: 8 minutes
Nutritional Value: Rich in flavor and high-quality protein.

Instant Pot Mushroom and Spinach Risotto

Ingredients:
- 1 cup Arborio rice
- 2 cups mushrooms, sliced
- 4 cups vegetable broth
- 1 onion, diced
- 2 cloves garlic, minced

- 1/2 cup dry white wine
- 2 tablespoons olive oil
- Salt and pepper to taste
- Grated Parmesan cheese for garnish

Instructions:

- Set Instant Pot to "Sauté" and cook onion and garlic in olive oil until softened.
- Add mushrooms and continue to sauté until browned.
- Pour in Arborio rice and stir.
- Deglaze with white wine, then add vegetable broth, salt, and pepper.
- Set to "Manual" for 6 minutes.
- Quick release and serve with grated Parmesan cheese.

Prep Time: 20 minutes
Cook Time: 6 minutes
Nutritional Value: Creamy and satisfying with a rich umami flavor.

CHAPTER 4: APPETIZERS SOUPS AND SIDES

Instant Pot Spinach and Artichoke Dip

Ingredients:
- 1 cup frozen spinach, thawed and drained
- 1 can artichoke hearts, chopped
- 1 cup cream cheese, softened
- 1 cup sour cream
- 1 cup shredded mozzarella cheese
- 1/2 cup grated Parmesan cheese
- 2 cloves garlic, minced
- Salt and pepper to taste
- Tortilla chips for serving

Instructions:
- In the Instant Pot, mix together spinach, artichoke hearts, cream cheese, sour cream, mozzarella cheese, Parmesan cheese, garlic, salt, and pepper.

- Set to "Sauté" and cook until the cheeses are melted.

Serve warm with tortilla chips.
Prep Time: 10 minutes
Cook Time: 5 minutes
Nutritional Value: Rich in calcium and antioxidants.

Instant Pot Tomato Basil Soup

Ingredients:
- 1 can diced tomatoes
- 1 onion, diced
- 2 cloves garlic, minced
- 4 cups vegetable broth
- 1 cup fresh basil leaves
- 1/2 cup heavy cream
- Salt and pepper to taste
- Croutons for garnish

Instructions:
- In the Instant Pot, combine diced tomatoes, onion, garlic, vegetable broth, and basil.
- Set to "Soup" mode for 10 minutes.

- Use an immersion blender to puree the soup.
- Stir in heavy cream, salt, and pepper.
- Serve hot with croutons.

Prep Time: 15 minutes
Cook Time: 10 minutes
Nutritional Value: High in vitamin C and antioxidants.

Instant Pot Buffalo Cauliflower Bites

Ingredients:
- 1 head cauliflower, cut into florets
- 1/2 cup buffalo sauce
- 1/4 cup melted butter
- 1 teaspoon garlic powder
- 1 teaspoon onion powder
- 1/2 teaspoon smoked paprika
- Ranch dressing for dipping

Instructions:

- In the Instant Pot, toss cauliflower florets with buffalo sauce, melted

butter, garlic powder, onion powder, and smoked paprika.
- Set to "Manual" for 3 minutes.
- Quick release and serve with ranch dressing.

Prep Time: 10 minutes
Cook Time: 3 minutes
Nutritional Value: Low in calories and a good source of fiber.

Instant Pot Loaded Baked Potato Soup

Ingredients:
- 4 potatoes, peeled and diced
- 1 onion, diced
- 2 cloves garlic, minced
- 4 cups chicken broth
- 1 cup shredded cheddar cheese
- 1/2 cup sour cream
- 1/4 cup chopped green onions
- Bacon bits for garnish

Instructions:

- In the Instant Pot, combine potatoes, onion, garlic, and chicken broth.
- Set to "Soup" mode for 8 minutes.
- Use a fork to mash some of the potatoes.
- Stir in cheddar cheese, sour cream, and green onions.
- Serve hot, garnished with bacon bits.

Prep Time: 15 minutes
Cook Time: 8 minutes
Nutritional Value: Comforting and rich in calcium.

Instant Pot Caprese Salad Skewers

Ingredients:
- 1 pint cherry tomatoes
- 1 package fresh mozzarella balls
- Fresh basil leaves
- Balsamic glaze for drizzling
- Toothpicks for assembling

Instructions:

- Assemble cherry tomatoes, mozzarella balls, and basil leaves on toothpicks.
- Arrange the skewers in the Instant Pot.
- Set to "Steam" for 2 minutes.
- Drizzle with balsamic glaze before serving.

Prep Time: 10 minutes
Cook Time: 2 minutes
Nutritional Value: Low-calorie and high in antioxidants.

Instant Pot Garlic Parmesan Brussels Sprouts

Ingredients:
- 1 lb Brussels sprouts, halved
- 1/4 cup grated Parmesan cheese
- 2 tablespoons olive oil
- 2 cloves garlic, minced
- Salt and pepper to taste
- Lemon wedges for serving

Instructions:

- In the Instant Pot, toss Brussels sprouts with Parmesan cheese, olive oil, garlic, salt, and pepper.
- Set to "Manual" for 3 minutes.
- Quick release and squeeze lemon wedges over the top before serving.

Prep Time: 15 minutes
Cook Time: 3 minutes
Nutritional Value: High in fiber and vitamin C

Instant Pot Creamy Corn Dip

Ingredients:
- 2 cups corn kernels
- 1 cup cream cheese, softened
- 1 cup shredded cheddar cheese
- 1/2 cup mayonnaise
- 1/4 cup chopped green onions
- 1/4 cup chopped jalapeños (optional)
- 1 teaspoon garlic powder
- Tortilla chips for serving

Instructions:

- In the Instant Pot, mix together corn, cream cheese, cheddar cheese, mayonnaise, green onions, jalapeños, and garlic powder.
- Set to "Sauté" and cook until the cheeses are melted.

Serve warm with tortilla chips.
Prep Time: 10 minutes
Cook Time: 5 minutes
Nutritional Value: Creamy and satisfying.

Instant Pot Sweet Potato Fries

Ingredients:
- 2 large sweet potatoes, cut into fries
- 2 tablespoons olive oil
- 1 teaspoon paprika
- 1/2 teaspoon garlic powder
- 1/2 teaspoon cumin
- Salt and pepper to taste
- Fresh parsley for garnish

Instructions:

- Toss sweet potato fries with olive oil, paprika, garlic powder, cumin, salt, and pepper in the Instant Pot.
- Set to "Manual" for 5 minutes.
- Quick release and garnish with fresh parsley.

Prep Time: 15 minutes
Cook Time: 5 minutes
Nutritional Value: High in beta-carotene and fiber.

Instant Pot Greek Salad

Ingredients:
- 2 cucumbers, diced
- 1 pint cherry tomatoes, halved
- 1 cup Kalamata olives, pitted
- 1/2 cup red onion, thinly sliced
- 1 cup feta cheese, crumbled
- 1/4 cup olive oil
- 2 tablespoons red wine vinegar
- 1 teaspoon dried oregano
- Salt and pepper to taste

Instructions:

- In the Instant Pot, combine cucumbers, cherry tomatoes, olives, red onion, and feta cheese.
- In a small bowl, combine the olive oil, red wine vinegar, dried oregano, salt, and pepper.
- Pour the dressing over the salad and gently mix before serving.

Prep Time: 15 minutes
Cook Time: 0 minutes
Nutritional Value: High in antioxidants and healthy fats.

Instant Pot Buttery Garlic Knots

Ingredients:
- 1 lb pizza dough
- 1/2 cup unsalted butter, melted
- 3 cloves garlic, minced
- 1/4 cup chopped parsley
- Salt to taste
- Marinara sauce for dipping

Instructions:

- Roll pizza dough into small ropes and tie into knots.
- In the Instant Pot, mix melted butter, minced garlic, chopped parsley, and salt.
- Place the knots in the Instant Pot and coat with the garlic butter mixture.
- Set to "Manual" for 5 minutes.
- Serve with marinara sauce for dipping.

Prep Time: 20 minutes

Cook Time: 5 minutes

Nutritional Value: Soft and flavorful, a perfect appetizer or side.

Chapter 5: Vegan and Vegetarian

Instant Pot Lentil Soup (Vegan)

Ingredients:
- 1 cup dried green lentils, rinsed
- 4 cups vegetable broth
- 1 onion, diced
- 2 carrots, sliced
- 2 celery stalks, chopped
- 2 cloves garlic, minced
- 1 teaspoon cumin
- 1 teaspoon smoked paprika
- Salt and pepper to taste
- Fresh parsley for garnish

Instructions:
- Combine lentils, vegetable broth, onion, carrots, celery, garlic, cumin, smoked paprika, salt, and pepper in the Instant Pot.
- Set to "Soup" mode for 15 minutes.

- Natural pressure release and garnish with fresh parsley.

Prep Time: 10 minutes
Cook Time: 15 minutes
Nutritional Value: High in protein, fiber, and essential nutrients.

Instant Pot Chickpea and Spinach Curry (Vegan)

Ingredients:
- 2 cans chickpeas, drained and rinsed
- 1 onion, diced
- 2 tomatoes, diced
- 2 cups fresh spinach
- 1 can coconut milk
- 2 tablespoons curry powder
- 1 teaspoon turmeric
- 1 teaspoon cumin
- Salt and pepper to taste
- Fresh cilantro for garnish

Instructions:

- In the Instant Pot, combine chickpeas, onion, tomatoes, spinach, coconut milk, curry powder, turmeric, cumin, salt, and pepper.
- Set to "Manual" for 5 minutes.
- Quick release and garnish with fresh cilantro.

Prep Time: 15 minutes
Cook Time: 5 minutes
Nutritional Value: Plant-based and rich in protein.

Instant Pot Vegetable Paella (Vegetarian)

Ingredients:
- 1 cup Arborio rice
- 2 cups vegetable broth
- 1 onion, diced
- 1 bell pepper, sliced
- 1 zucchini, diced
- 1 cup cherry tomatoes, halved
- 1/2 cup frozen peas
- 2 cloves garlic, minced

- 1 teaspoon smoked paprika
- 1/2 teaspoon saffron threads (optional)
- Salt and pepper to taste
- Lemon wedges for serving

Instructions:
- Combine Arborio rice, vegetable broth, onion, bell pepper, zucchini, cherry tomatoes, peas, garlic, smoked paprika, saffron threads, salt, and pepper in the Instant Pot.
- Set to "Manual" for 6 minutes.
- Quickly release the rice and fluff it with a fork.
- Serve with lemon wedges.

Prep Time: 20 minutes
Cook Time: 6 minutes
Nutritional Value: A colorful and flavorful vegetarian dish.

Instant Pot Black Bean Chili (Vegan)

Ingredients:

- 2 cans black beans, drained and rinsed
- 1 can diced tomatoes
- 1 onion, diced
- 2 bell peppers, diced
- 2 cloves garlic, minced
- 2 tablespoons chili powder
- 1 teaspoon cumin
- 1 teaspoon smoked paprika
- Salt and pepper to taste
- Avocado and cilantro for topping

Instructions:
- Combine black beans, diced tomatoes, onion, bell peppers, garlic, chili powder, cumin, smoked paprika, salt, and pepper in the Instant Pot.
- Set to "Manual" for 10 minutes.
- Quick release and serve with sliced avocado and cilantro.

Prep Time: 15 minutes
Cook Time: 10 minutes
Nutritional Value: High in protein, fiber, and antioxidants.

Instant Pot Eggplant and Chickpea Stew (Vegan)

Ingredients:
- 1 eggplant, diced
- 1 can chickpeas, drained and rinsed
- 1 onion, diced
- 2 bell peppers, sliced
- 2 cups tomato sauce
- 2 cloves garlic, minced
- 1 teaspoon cumin
- 1 teaspoon smoked paprika
- Salt and pepper to taste
- Fresh parsley for garnish

Instructions:
- Combine eggplant, chickpeas, onion, bell peppers, tomato sauce, garlic, cumin, smoked paprika, salt, and pepper in the Instant Pot.
- Set to "Manual" for 8 minutes.
- Quick release and garnish with fresh parsley before serving.

Prep Time: 15 minutes
Cook Time: 8 minutes
Nutritional Value: Plant-based and rich in fiber.

Instant Pot Quinoa and Vegetable Stir-Fry (Vegetarian)

Ingredients:
- 1 cup quinoa, rinsed
- 2 cups vegetable broth
- 1 onion, sliced
- 1 bell pepper, sliced
- 1 zucchini, sliced
- 1 carrot, julienned
- 2 tablespoons soy sauce
- 1 tablespoon sesame oil
- 1 teaspoon ginger, grated
- 2 cloves garlic, minced
- Green onions for garnish

Instructions:
- Combine quinoa, vegetable broth, onion, bell pepper, zucchini, carrot,

soy sauce, sesame oil, ginger, and garlic in the Instant Pot.
- Set to "Manual" for 2 minutes.
- Quick release and garnish with green onions.

Prep Time: 20 minutes
Cook Time: 2 minutes
Nutritional Value: Protein-packed and full of colorful vegetables.

Instant Pot Sweet Potato and Chickpea Curry (Vegan)

Ingredients:
- 2 sweet potatoes, diced
- 1 can chickpeas, drained and rinsed
- 1 onion, diced
- 1 can coconut milk
- 2 tablespoons curry powder
- 1 teaspoon turmeric
- 1 teaspoon cumin
- 2 cloves garlic, minced
- Salt and pepper to taste
- Fresh cilantro for garnish

Instructions:
- Combine sweet potatoes, chickpeas, onion, coconut milk, curry powder, turmeric, cumin, garlic, salt, and pepper in the Instant Pot.
- Set to "Manual" for 5 minutes.
- Quick release and garnish with fresh cilantro.

Prep Time: 15 minutes
Cook Time: 5 minutes
Nutritional Value: Rich in vitamins and plant-based protein.

Instant Pot Mushroom Risotto (Vegetarian)

Ingredients:
- 1 cup Arborio rice
- 2 cups mushrooms, sliced
- 4 cups vegetable broth
- 1 onion, diced
- 2 cloves garlic, minced
- 1/2 cup dry white wine
- 2 tablespoons olive oil

- Salt and pepper to taste
- Grated Parmesan cheese for garnish

Instructions:
- Set Instant Pot to "Sauté" and cook onion and garlic in olive oil until softened.
- Add mushrooms and continue to sauté until browned.
- Pour in Arborio rice and stir.
- Deglaze with white wine, then add vegetable broth, salt, and pepper.
- Set to "Manual" for 6 minutes.
- Quick release and serve with grated Parmesan cheese.

Prep Time: 20 minutes
Cook Time: 6 minutes
Nutritional Value: Creamy and satisfying with a rich umami flavor.

Instant Pot Red Lentil Curry (Vegan)

Ingredients:

- 1 cup red lentils, rinsed
- 4 cups vegetable broth
- 1 onion, diced
- 2 tomatoes, diced
- 2 cups spinach leaves
- 2 tablespoons curry powder
- 1 teaspoon cumin
- 1 teaspoon turmeric
- 2 cloves garlic, minced
- Salt and pepper to taste
- Lemon wedges for serving

Instructions:
- Combine red lentils, vegetable broth, onion, tomatoes, spinach, curry powder, cumin, turmeric, garlic, salt, and pepper in the Instant Pot.
- Set to "Manual" for 8 minutes.
- Quick release and serve with lemon wedges.

Prep Time: 15 minutes
Cook Time: 8 minutes
Nutritional Value: High in protein, fiber, and iron.

Instant Pot Cauliflower and Chickpea Curry (Vegan)

Ingredients:
- 1 head cauliflower, cut into florets
- 1 can chickpeas, drained and rinsed
- 1 onion, diced
- 2 cloves garlic, minced
- 1 can diced tomatoes
- 1 can coconut milk
- 2 tablespoons curry powder
- 1 teaspoon turmeric
- Salt and pepper to taste
- Fresh cilantro for garnish

Instructions:
- Set Instant Pot to "Sauté" and cook onion and garlic until softened.
- Add cauliflower, chickpeas, diced tomatoes, coconut milk, curry powder, turmeric, salt, and pepper.
- Set to "Manual" for 5 minutes.
- Quick release and garnish with fresh cilantro.

Prep Time: 15 minutes

Cook Time: 5 minutes
Nutritional Value: Plant-based and rich in fiber.

Chapter 7

CHAPTER 6: FISH AND SEAFOODS

Instant Pot Lemon Garlic Butter Shrimp

Ingredients:
- 1 lb large shrimp, peeled and deveined
- 1/2 cup unsalted butter, melted
- 3 cloves garlic, minced
- 2 tablespoons lemon juice
- 1 teaspoon dried parsley
- Salt and pepper to taste
- Fresh parsley for garnish

Instructions:
- In the Instant Pot, combine shrimp, melted butter, minced garlic, lemon juice, dried parsley, salt, and pepper.
- Set to "Manual" for 2 minutes.
- Quick release and garnish with fresh parsley before serving.

Prep Time: 10 minutes

Cook Time: 2 minutes

Nutritional Value: High in protein and omega-3 fatty acids.

Instant Pot Garlic Herb Salmon

Ingredients:
- 4 salmon filets
- 1/4 cup olive oil
- 3 cloves garlic, minced
- 1 teaspoon dried thyme
- 1 teaspoon dried rosemary
- 1 teaspoon dried parsley
- Salt and pepper to taste
- Lemon wedges for serving

Instructions:
- In a bowl, mix olive oil, minced garlic, thyme, rosemary, parsley, salt, and pepper.
- Place salmon filets in the Instant Pot and pour the herb mixture over them.
- Set to "Manual" for 3 minutes.
- Quick release and serve with lemon wedges.

Prep Time: 10 minutes
Cook Time: 3 minutes
Nutritional Value: Rich in omega-3 fatty acids.

Instant Pot Cajun Shrimp and Sausage Jambalaya

Ingredients:
- 1 lb shrimp, peeled and deveined
- 1 lb Andouille sausage, sliced
- 1 onion, diced
- 1 bell pepper, diced
- 2 celery stalks, chopped
- 3 cloves garlic, minced
- 1 can diced tomatoes
- 1 cup long-grain rice
- 2 cups chicken broth
- 2 teaspoons Cajun seasoning
- Salt and pepper to taste
- Green onions for garnish

Instructions:

- In the Instant Pot, combine shrimp, sausage, onion, bell pepper, celery, garlic, diced tomatoes, rice, chicken broth, Cajun seasoning, salt, and pepper.
- Set to "Manual" for 5 minutes.
- Quick release and garnish with green onions.

Prep Time: 20 minutes
Cook Time: 5 minutes
Nutritional Value: Protein-rich and full of savory flavors.

Instant Pot Coconut-Lime Cod Fish Tacos

Ingredients:
- 1 lb cod filets
- 1 can coconut milk
- 2 limes, juiced
- 2 teaspoons ground cumin
- 1 teaspoon chili powder
- 1 teaspoon garlic powder
- Salt and pepper to taste

- Corn tortillas for serving
- Cabbage slaw for topping

Instructions:
- In the Instant Pot, place cod filets and pour coconut milk over them.
- Add lime juice, ground cumin, chili powder, garlic powder, salt, and pepper.
- Set to "Manual" for 4 minutes.
- Quick release and serve the cod in corn tortillas with cabbage slaw.

Prep Time: 15 minutes
Cook Time: 4 minutes
Nutritional Value: Light and refreshing with a tropical twist.

Instant Pot Seafood Paella

Ingredients:
- 1 cup Arborio rice
- 1 lb mixed seafood (shrimp, mussels, squid)
- 1 onion, diced
- 1 bell pepper, sliced

- 2 tomatoes, diced
- 2 cloves garlic, minced
- 1 teaspoon smoked paprika
- 1/2 teaspoon saffron threads (optional)
- 2 cups fish broth
- Salt and pepper to taste
- Lemon wedges for serving

Instructions:

- Combine Arborio rice, mixed seafood, onion, bell pepper, tomatoes, garlic, smoked paprika, saffron threads, fish broth, salt, and pepper in the Instant Pot.
- Set to "Manual" for 6 minutes.
- Quick release and serve with lemon wedges.

Prep Time: 20 minutes
Cook Time: 6 minutes
Nutritional Value: A flavorful and hearty seafood dish.

Instant Pot Teriyaki Salmon Bowl

Ingredients:
- 4 salmon filets
- 1/2 cup soy sauce
- 1/4 cup honey
- 2 tablespoons rice vinegar
- 1 tablespoon ginger, grated
- 2 cloves garlic, minced
- 1 tablespoon cornstarch
- Sesame seeds and green onions for garnish
- Cooked rice for serving

Instructions:
- Place salmon filets in the Instant Pot.
- In a bowl, mix soy sauce, honey, rice vinegar, ginger, garlic, and cornstarch.
- Pour the sauce over the salmon.
- Set to "Manual" for 3 minutes.
- Quick release and serve over cooked rice, garnished with sesame seeds and green onions.

Prep Time: 15 minutes
Cook Time: 3 minutes

Nutritional Value: Sweet and savory, high in omega-3 fatty acids.

Instant Pot Garlic Lemon Butter Scallops

Ingredients:
- 1 lb scallops
- 1/2 cup unsalted butter, melted
- 3 cloves garlic, minced
- Zest of 1 lemon
- Juice of 1 lemon
- 1 teaspoon dried parsley
- Salt and pepper to taste

Instructions:
- In the Instant Pot, combine scallops, melted butter, minced garlic, lemon zest, lemon juice, dried parsley, salt, and pepper.
- Set to "Manual" for 1 minute.
- Quick release and serve immediately.

Prep Time: 10 minutes
Cook Time: 1 minute

Nutritional Value: Rich in protein and a burst of citrus flavor.

Instant Pot Thai Coconut Shrimp Soup

Ingredients:
- 1 lb shrimp, peeled and deveined
- 1 can coconut milk
- 3 cups vegetable broth
- 1 red bell pepper, sliced
- 1 carrot, julienned
- 2 tablespoons Thai red curry paste
- 1 tablespoon fish sauce (optional for non-vegetarian version)
- 2 teaspoons brown sugar
- 2 cloves garlic, minced
- Rice noodles for serving
- Fresh cilantro for garnish

Instructions:
- In the Instant Pot, combine shrimp, coconut milk, vegetable broth, red bell pepper, carrot, Thai red curry paste,

fish sauce (if using), brown sugar, and minced garlic.
- Set to "Soup" mode for 5 minutes.
- Quick release and serve over rice noodles, garnished with fresh cilantro.

Prep Time: 20 minutes
Cook Time: 5 minutes
Nutritional Value: A comforting and aromatic seafood soup.

Instant Pot Lemon Dill Cod Filets

Ingredients:
- 4 cod filets
- 1/4 cup olive oil
- 3 tablespoons lemon juice
- 2 tablespoons fresh dill, chopped
- 2 cloves garlic, minced
- Salt and pepper to taste
- Lemon slices for garnish

Instructions:
- Place cod filets in the Instant Pot.

- In a bowl, mix olive oil, lemon juice, chopped dill, minced garlic, salt, and pepper.
- Pour the mixture over the cod.
- Set to "Manual" for 3 minutes.
- Quick release and serve with lemon slices.

Prep Time: 15 minutes
Cook Time: 3 minutes
Nutritional Value: Light and flavorful, a perfect dish for lemon and dill lovers.

Instant Pot Spicy Garlic Butter Lobster Tails

Ingredients:
- 4 lobster tails, thawed
- 1/2 cup unsalted butter, melted
- 3 cloves garlic, minced
- 1 teaspoon red pepper flakes
- 1 teaspoon smoked paprika
- Salt and pepper to taste
- Fresh parsley for garnish

Instructions:

- In the Instant Pot, place lobster tails.
- In a bowl, mix melted butter, minced garlic, red pepper flakes, smoked paprika, salt, and pepper.
- Pour the garlic butter mixture over the lobster tails.
- Set to "Manual" for 2 minutes.
- Quick release and garnish with fresh parsley before serving.

Prep Time: 20 minutes
Cook Time: 2 minutes
Nutritional Value: Indulgent and spicy, a seafood delight.

CHAPTER 7: DESSERT AND DRINKS

Instant Pot Chocolate Lava Cake

Ingredients:
- 1 cup all-purpose flour
- 1/2 cup unsweetened cocoa powder
- 1 cup granulated sugar
- 1/2 cup milk
- 1/4 cup melted butter
- 1 teaspoon vanilla extract
- 1/4 teaspoon salt
- 1 cup hot water

Instructions:
- In a bowl, whisk together flour, cocoa powder, sugar, milk, melted butter, vanilla extract, and salt.
- Grease the Instant Pot insert and pour the batter into it.
- In a separate bowl, mix hot water and sugar, then pour it over the batter in the Instant Pot.

- Set to "Manual" for 15 minutes.
- Natural pressure releases and is warm.

Prep Time: 10 minutes
Cook Time: 15 minutes
Nutritional Value: Rich and indulgent, a perfect chocolatey treat.

Instant Pot Vanilla Rice Pudding

Ingredients:
- 1 cup Arborio rice
- 4 cups milk
- 1/2 cup granulated sugar
- 1 teaspoon vanilla extract
- 1/2 teaspoon ground cinnamon
- Pinch of salt
- Raisins (optional)

Instructions:
- Combine Arborio rice, milk, sugar, vanilla extract, cinnamon, and salt in the Instant Pot.
- Set to "Porridge" mode for 20 minutes.

- Natural pressure release and stir in raisins if desired.
- Serve warm or chilled.

Prep Time: 5 minutes
Cook Time: 20 minutes
Nutritional Value: Creamy and comforting, a classic dessert.

Instant Pot Apple Crisp

Ingredients:
- 4 cups sliced apples
- 1 tablespoon lemon juice
- 1/2 cup rolled oats
- 1/2 cup all-purpose flour
- 1/2 cup brown sugar
- 1/4 cup melted butter
- 1 teaspoon ground cinnamon
- 1/4 teaspoon nutmeg
- Vanilla ice cream for serving

Instructions:
- Toss sliced apples with lemon juice and place them in the Instant Pot.

- In a bowl, combine rolled oats, flour, brown sugar, melted butter, cinnamon, and nutmeg.
- Sprinkle the oat mixture over the apples in the Instant Pot.
- Set to "Manual" for 8 minutes.
- Quick release and serve with a scoop of vanilla ice cream.

Prep Time: 15 minutes
Cook Time: 8 minutes
Nutritional Value: Warm and spiced, a delightful apple dessert.

Instant Pot Chocolate Cheesecake

Ingredients:
- 1 1/2 cups chocolate cookie crumbs
- 1/4 cup melted butter
- 3 packages (24 oz) cream cheese, softened
- 1 cup granulated sugar
- 1/2 cup cocoa powder
- 3 large eggs
- 1 cup sour cream
- 1 teaspoon vanilla extract

- Chocolate ganache for topping

Instructions:
- Mix chocolate cookie crumbs with melted butter and press into the base of a springform pan to create the crust.
- In a bowl, beat cream cheese, sugar, and cocoa powder until smooth.
- Add the eggs one at a time, beating well after each addition.
- Stir in sour cream and vanilla extract.
- Pour the mixture into the prepared crust.
- Cover the pan with foil and place it on the Instant Pot trivet.
- Add 1 cup of water to the Instant Pot, place the trivet with the cheesecake inside, and set to "Manual" for 35 minutes.
- Natural pressure release, then refrigerate the cheesecake for at least 4 hours.
- Top with chocolate ganache before serving.

Prep Time: 20 minutes
Cook Time: 35 minutes (+ chilling time)
Nutritional Value: Rich and decadent, a chocolate lover's dream.

Instant Pot Lemon Blueberry Bread Pudding

Ingredients:
- 6 cups cubed bread
- 1 cup fresh or frozen blueberries
- 4 large eggs
- 1 1/2 cups milk
- 1/2 cup granulated sugar
- 1/4 cup melted butter
- 1 teaspoon vanilla extract
- Zest of 1 lemon
- Powdered sugar for dusting

Instructions:
- Grease the Instant Pot insert and place cubed bread and blueberries inside.

- In a bowl, whisk together eggs, milk, sugar, melted butter, vanilla extract, and lemon zest.
- Pour the egg mixture onto the bread and blueberries.
- Set to "Manual" for 20 minutes.
- Natural pressure release and dust with powdered sugar before serving.

Prep Time: 15 minutes
Cook Time: 20 minutes
Nutritional Value: Fruity and tangy, a twist on classic bread pudding.

Instant Pot Pumpkin Spice Rice Pudding

Ingredients:
- 1 cup Arborio rice
- 4 cups milk
- 1 cup canned pumpkin puree
- 1/2 cup brown sugar
- 1 teaspoon pumpkin pie spice
- 1/2 teaspoon vanilla extract
- Pinch of salt
- Whipped cream for topping

Instructions:

- Combine Arborio rice, milk, pumpkin puree, brown sugar, pumpkin pie spice, vanilla extract, and salt in the Instant Pot.
- Set to "Porridge" mode for 20 minutes.
- Natural pressure release and stir well.
- Serve warm, topped with whipped cream.

Prep Time: 10 minutes
Cook Time: 20 minutes
Nutritional Value: Creamy and spiced, a fall-inspired dessert.

Instant Pot Cherry Almond Clafoutis

Ingredients:
- 2 cups fresh or frozen cherries, pitted
- 1/2 cup almond flour
- 1/2 cup all-purpose flour
- 1/2 cup granulated sugar
- 1/4 teaspoon salt
- 3 large eggs

- 1 1/2 cups milk
- 1 teaspoon almond extract
- Powdered sugar for dusting

Instructions:
- Grease the Instant Pot insert and place cherries inside.
- In a bowl, whisk together almond flour, all-purpose flour, sugar, and salt.
- In another bowl, beat eggs, then add milk and almond extract.
- Whisk the dry ingredients into the wet until smooth.
- Pour the batter over the cherries in the Instant Pot.
- Set to "Manual" for 25 minutes.
- Natural pressure release and dust with powdered sugar before serving.

Prep Time: 15 minutes
Cook Time: 25 minutes
Nutritional Value: Nutty and fruity, a delightful French dessert.

Instant Pot Caramel Pecan Cheesecake

Ingredients:
- 1 1/2 cups graham cracker crumbs
- 1/2 cup melted butter
- 3 packages (24 oz) cream cheese, softened
- 1 cup granulated sugar
- 3 large eggs
- 1/2 cup sour cream
- 1 teaspoon vanilla extract
- 1 cup caramel sauce
- 1 cup chopped pecans

Instructions:
- Mix graham cracker crumbs with melted butter and press into the base of a springform pan to create the crust.
- In a mixing dish, combine cream cheese and sugar and beat until smooth.
- Add the eggs one at a time, beating well after each addition.

- Stir in the sour cream and vanilla extract.
- Pour half of the cream cheese mixture onto the crust.
- Drizzle half of the caramel sauce and sprinkle half of the chopped pecans.
- Repeat with the remaining cream cheese mixture, caramel sauce, and chopped pecans.
- Cover the pan with foil and place it on the Instant Pot trivet.
- Add 1 cup of water to the Instant Pot, place the trivet with the cheesecake inside, and set to "Manual" for 35 minutes.
- Natural pressure release, then refrigerate the cheesecake for at least 4 hours.
- Prep Time: 25 minutes

Cook Time: 35 minutes (+ chilling time)
Nutritional Value: Sweet and nutty, a caramel lover's delight.

Instant Pot Mint Chocolate Cheesecake

Ingredients:
- 1 1/2 cups chocolate cookie crumbs
- 1/4 cup melted butter
- 3 packages (24 oz) cream cheese, softened
- 1 cup granulated sugar
- 3 large eggs
- 1/2 cup sour cream
- 1 teaspoon peppermint extract
- Green food coloring (optional)
- 1 cup chocolate chips
- Mint leaves for garnish

Instructions:
- Mix chocolate cookie crumbs with melted butter and press into the base of a springform pan to create the crust.
- Beat the cream cheese and sugar together in a mixing basin until creamy.

- Add the eggs one at a time, beating thoroughly after each addition.
- Stir in sour cream, peppermint extract, and green food coloring (if using).
- Fold in chocolate chips.
- Pour the mixture over the crust.
- Cover the pan with foil and place it on the Instant Pot trivet.
- Add 1 cup of water to the Instant Pot, place the trivet with the cheesecake inside, and set to "Manual" for 35 minutes.
- Natural pressure release, then refrigerate the cheesecake for at least 4 hours.
- Garnish with mint leaves before serving.

Prep Time: 25 minutes
Cook Time: 35 minutes (+ chilling time)
Nutritional Value: Refreshing and chocolaty, a perfect combination.

Instant Pot Iced Caramel Macchiato

Ingredients:
- 1 cup strong brewed coffee, cooled
- 1/2 cup milk
- 2 tablespoons caramel syrup
- 1 tablespoon vanilla syrup
- Ice cubes

Instructions:
- In a glass, combine cooled brewed coffee, milk, caramel syrup, and vanilla syrup.
- Fill another glass with ice cubes.
- Pour the coffee mixture over the ice.
- Stir well and enjoy your homemade iced caramel macchiato.

Prep Time: 5 minutes
Cook Time: 0 minutes
Nutritional Value: A refreshing and sweet coffee treat.

CONCLUSION

Congratulations on embarking on the thrilling adventure of mastering your Instant Pot! This versatile kitchen companion has undoubtedly revolutionized the way you approach cooking, providing you with the efficiency and convenience that every modern home chef craves. As you conclude your culinary journey with the Instant Pot, reflect on the skills you've acquired, the delicious meals you've crafted, and the newfound confidence you've gained in the kitchen.

Unleashing the Magic of Instant Pot Cooking

Throughout this cookbook, you've delved into the intricacies of Instant Pot cooking, discovering its incredible capacity to transform raw ingredients into delectable dishes in record time. The Instant Pot has proved to be more than just a kitchen appliance; it's a culinary wizard that effortlessly combines speed, flavor, and nutrition. From breakfast to dinner, appetizers to desserts, your Instant Pot has become an indispensable ally, simplifying complex recipes and empowering you to experiment with a diverse range of cuisines.

A Symphony of Flavors and Textures

One of the most captivating aspects of Instant Pot cooking is its ability to marry flavors and textures harmoniously. Whether you've indulged in hearty stews, succulent meats, or vibrant vegetables, the Instant Pot's sealed cooking environment ensures that every ingredient absorbs the essence of the dish, resulting in a symphony of flavors that dance across your tongue.The tender meats, perfectly cooked grains, and rich sauces all bear witness to the culinary mastery you've achieved.

Time-Saving Elegance

Time is a precious commodity, and the Instant Pot has proven to be the ultimate time-saving tool for the busy home cook. With pressure cooking, slow cooking, sautéing, and more, all consolidated into a single device, you've reclaimed hours in your day without compromising on the quality of your meals. The Instant Pot has effortlessly bridged the gap between fast food and gourmet dining, allowing you to whip up impressive dishes even on the busiest of days.

Confidence in the Kitchen

As you've progressed through this cookbook, you've undoubtedly developed a newfound confidence in the kitchen. No longer intimidated by intricate recipes or lengthy cooking times, you now approach each meal with the assurance that the Instant Pot has your back. Your understanding of cooking principles, ingredient combinations, and Instant Pot techniques has elevated you to the status of a culinary maestro. The once-daunting prospect of preparing elaborate meals is now a thrilling challenge you eagerly embrace.

Navigating the Instant Pot Terrain

Navigating the terrain of Instant Pot cooking involves not only mastering the basic functions but also experimenting with different settings, cooking times, and pressure levels. As you conclude this culinary journey, take pride in the fact that you've become a proficient navigator of the Instant Pot landscape. You've learned to decipher the language of beeps, understand the significance of quick release versus natural release, and adapt recipes to suit your taste and dietary preferences.

A Toolbox of Techniques

Your journey with the Instant Pot has equipped you with a toolbox of techniques that extend beyond pressure cooking. Sautéing, steaming, and slow cooking are just a few of the versatile methods you've embraced. The Instant Pot's ability to replace multiple kitchen appliances has streamlined your cooking process, minimizing cleanup and maximizing efficiency. You're now adept at choosing the right technique for each culinary endeavor, ensuring that your meals are not only delicious but also prepared with finesse.

Resources and Further Reading

As you conclude this cookbook, remember that your culinary education is a continuous journey. The resources and further reading provided here are invaluable companions on your quest for culinary excellence. Consider exploring additional cookbooks dedicated to Instant Pot mastery, as well as online communities and forums where you can share experiences, swap recipes, and learn from fellow Instant Pot enthusiasts.

The Culinary Adventure Continues

As you bid farewell to this cookbook, remember that your Instant Pot is a gateway to endless culinary possibilities. The skills you've acquired are the foundation for a lifetime of delicious discoveries in the kitchen. Continue to experiment, innovate, and savor the joy of creating mouthwatering meals for yourself and your loved ones.

The culinary adventure doesn't end here; it evolves. So, don your apron, embrace the artistry of cooking, and let your Instant Pot continue to be the catalyst for culinary brilliance in your home.

Happy cooking!!

Printed in Great Britain
by Amazon